SIXTY POEMS

Loretta Moore

ISBN: 978-81-8253-867-2

First Edition: 2022
Rs. 200/-

Cyberwit.net
HIG 45 Kaushambi Kunj, Kalindipuram
Allahabad - 211011 (U.P.) India
http://www.cyberwit.net
Tel: +(91) 9415091004
E-mail: info@cyberwit.net

Contents

"Thinking Openly"

I was in a capsule of innocence and willingness…
It was a period of the undisclosed future,
before the schisms and failure, waiting-
I now find myself at those locations,
having traveled to those paths.
Curiously, nothing warns of life's true
difficulties ahead, the past holds a re-
collection of innocent light, glimpses inside
that timid horizon. Wistful and yearning and
sorrow-filled, I turn to mystery in a
bold atmosphere prepared to hurl at pleasure,
to instances recessed in my prior joyous
time.
The indefinable adversarial force idles, while
I appeal to the disrespectful goal present in living to STOP!
Take me to a superior moment, a realm of
superb reason, from this place trapping hollowness…
I'll put my arms snuggly around peace and
truth, a grain in the wilderness of life.

"The Freed Spirit"

The crush of life pounds my heart, I
seek the living blood and guts
of forsaken love...life's true spirit.
The haunted soul has strayed in areas-antici-
pating the heap and heft of living to come
and conquer all of me, in my desperate
search for the freed spirit.
In experience' corners, I've felt its wealth
and worth, and saw beyond all that it has for me...
Before I lose the pearl hailing me with romance
and serenades, I'm wistful elusion is not a fixture,
with discovery joining happiness and
the freed spirit and me.

"Life Explains Itself"

He lives in a past composed of Blues, a land
of songs that don't apply…and I cannot be
persuaded…
I was in open, broad spaces, on a lonely plain
for the encounter, when he happened by…..
In reality, I mistook a raw, rugged course
for sunny, smiling country love.
I have since lived with a falsified dream of
innocence floating on a barge of Hope,
a remembrance of romantic wishes disa-
ppoints on waves of the realness of life,
reference to existence is dreaded and disturbing,
absolute assuredness is stored away in memory
well-spent.
There are no gleaming horizons, no mountains
of certitude, evidence is in dismembered,
fractured hopes and dreams. Along with frailty I sit
in the pale moonlight, while heavily I cast my eye on life.

THE HUNT FOR JOY

Long, lonely stretches of time install the
the ground-level experience, pulling back
images of life…the peaceful long-haul.
The forgotten magical passage, the major
movement lies in a soothing, memorable past
longing to be loosed from all contractual dejections
and disappointments and insecurities. Hope is to take
hold of the bargaining chip, the open door
to satisfying dreams and peaceful visions-
to stare into the prism concocted by the mind,
stranded on a walk beside green pastures, walks
along lonely streets shaped from misty innocence
and uncovered happiness.
Mistakenly, over-active imperatives cast a dim
view as to seek access in the hunt for joy.

"Composition Melancholy"

Loneliness is your strange cradle; lidless, estranged eyes, empty.
Horizons sparse, spread with vigilant tracts of distillation, discouragement.
A symbol of renegade posts; outposts, plains full-proofed with indifference and atmospheres with dark shadows and fluid shade.
Dejection, rejection, sentimentality, a thin ray of hope flushed away.
Uncrowned, drowned spirit. Hope will arrive like the dawn!

"A World's Song of Woe"

I hear the plaintive sound, a silent cry at dawn
burgeoning, carried through the dark day before....
the irreversible voice lifting life and worldly
burdens from all 'round.....
keepers of earth's misery, seekers of seasonal
relief and calm....

"Living Magic"

A soft culture envelopes me….
the timeless, transient flow of
goodness and wholeness drawn
from breezy, blissful seasides and shores.
I surrender to wonders and magic
circulating in the atmosphere…the
ultimate, bottom-line uplift for humans is
punctuating life.

"Somber Shadows"

There's something magical and deep in somber
shadows—transformation covers the darkened
realm, revelation is somewhere in its midst-
the simplest structure, or measurable message
echoing its natural, mysterious depth.
It's a prolific sound deeply reflecting life.

"Appealing Structures"

There is something appealing about structures of seeming lesser value. This category in which there seems to be something of intense attraction manifested engages sites of barns, sheds and outbuildings and also covered bridges. There is a sort of shed which when I see it, seizes and holds my attention in its grasp. I am irrevocably attached to a particular outdoor storage shed that has many windows and is reddish in hue-faded, not new. It is pleasing every time I chance to find it standing in some backyard. There seems to be a correlation to a docked terribly-worn mariner's vessel as a New England shrimp boat, and there are other examples that I will not further provide. Perhaps all of these are comforting sightings for a spirit in this chaotic world. I seek those tracts of time for which there is no gage, just a soundless memory perpetuating the recognition of idyllic thought.

Spiritually Inspired Places

A spiritually inspired backdrop is where I often find myself. At those places, transferred by faith, I am in the presence of silence and peace. The sanctity of the Lord structurally resides on earth and throughout his creation as a source of restoration and His abundant love through spiritually inspired places.

Something in sunlight and shadows carries me to a peaceful background. It's a deep, private experience that suspends all logic and understanding, a natural, spiritually inherited place-God's Holy Light overwhelmingly sharing silence and peace, displaying His great love.

The following are but a few examples of spiritually inspired places God supplies:

Buildings and anything standing, desolate or deserted that darkened shadows have recessed and submerged; bright sunlight cruising a meadow or yard opening up a new day; a smile on baby's cherubic face; a pot or vase with flowers; a wall hanging painting, or mural; an appealing dog, cat, and other animals; a damask cloth covering a dining room table; shelved jars of foods home-canned; lights and lighting; placid meadows, farmland, and parks; streams, rivers, oceans, lakes.

The divinity of God transforms anything and everything by visions and images powerfully, serenely infiltrating spiritually, enhancing uplifting life on the this other dark, uninspired earth powerfully.

"Worlds We Choose"

We never live in chosen worlds-
they're make believe, serving dreams
on ice, frozen forevermore.....
No amount of happiness can end
a living reality.

"Sharing the Night"

I love communing with the wizened, mystical dark
transferring magic and secrets that traverse the cord
to earth from the awesome universe…
The monumental dark with stars sparkling bright….
its magic and power sharing the night…
Morning comes and nature's wilds whisper…
Tenderly, with birds in trees, softness comes
with every breeze, life is perfect, it's supreme,
my heartstring pulled by every river, pond and stream…

"A Billboard's Structure"

You glare with promise and sunny invitation propped up and pasted in towns and cities. As you stalk urban corners, and lonesome highways, your message is elastic, and sometimes broods beyond the picturesque images around hope. A plastic vision that creates dreams in vast surroundings, a silence escorting life, plastered on buildings or signs scrawled above wooden legs-the stilted, alienated forms-meandering with capitulated,
somber, bliss-filled messages spreading life and aspiration.

A Summer Night's Pleasure

We sat on the front steps he and I, truly a
summer pleasure....
In the darkness my sense of joy
reached remarkable measure...
My heart and thoughts rose as from leaven
those sumptuous warm nights beneath the dark heaven...
On the steps of our tiny, defunct dwelling looking above,
my transformed mind climbed roof-tops to a magical
star clad night sky and love...
Waves of Romance stole my young soul without a peep or sound,
with the deep darkness it had spread all around.

"Inch by Inch"

Inch by inch, little by little, Blacks have made their way toward equal status in America. In a landscape cluttered with hostility and opposition and uncertain acceptance, African Americans plowed their way through, and moved ahead. From Slavery, to Jim Crow and discrimination in various forms-some subtle, some overt-reaching the ultimate human goal has been accomplished, almost.

I yearn with all of my soul to be fully embraced, and whenever it occurs, filled with rapture my life shall be.

"The Creation of a Margin"

Lacking a direct point, it owns a distance from proper.
Equally away from lowly, from where it sits upon a fence,
With higher ambition, it searches for awareness while feeling
meager and staring through opaque lenses. Each step it takes
is critical, and seems a mockery.

"Black Melancholy"

Black melancholy in caves and dungeons, isolated
on rocky shores against which oceans of distant cries
bash and lash with gloom, doom.
Black melancholy hovering in monolithic, white-pillared
manors, in vast tear-filled fields and its sadness will loom.
Black melancholy fervently lamenting in melodies from
spirits of Blacks in crowded churches and jazz rooms.
Black millions following their dark tombs.

"Phenomenal Encounters"

They came as if from a deeply-intimate, remembered
The reenactment of some strange and
appealing space.. warm sightings and sensations.....
a living fresco, a mirror revealing memory from
distance and forgetfulness... condensation, revelations.
Everything transcribing poetic value, the truest relished
phenomena one's spiritual eyes could behold....

"Hinterland Woods"

White-clad woods I so desire, these spots I step into through
thought,
where wonderment in realms and worlds and texture I've found,
postured 'er I go, profound….
Winter scenes stored in hinterlands of time, worlds apart reach
my mind rejuvenated I, lost in a Writer's Lair…
my spirits rise, by all held captive in my eyes…nature revered, a
souls'
visions, images, input did repair…
Magic as in dreams is never as keen,
as this rapturous white-clad woods I've seen.

"A Childhood Wish"

It is regret I hold dear for childhood days
no longer here....
I'm sad that time past is so far from near.
The simple youth I used to know now seems bereft....
Wistfulness is gone, dreams're lost, lingering hope is left.

"The Goodness of Life"

There are places I enjoy strolling toward,
marvelous discoveries in a step I come upon
in an instance, with a glance-a solitary tree waves
its mystery and magic……..
Deep, the marrow of life that overturns earths'
lusciousness to reveal unexpected joy…….

"'The Bottom' Below My Window"

A galaxy of night transposed the deep darkness over the back-yard conveying inspiration to the row house on the narrow street where I lived as a child. The row house of my family hung in dejected surroundings with darkened parceled back yards. A moon's light lay over the darkness below my window in 'The Bottom' where I lived.

"Youth and Sun"

On those sunny days of my youth
life aimed for something far beyond
my natural being…In a rage of romantic
love and innocence, I stretched my arms
toward a cup of magic.

"You Made Me Lord"

YOU MADE ME, LORD…
YOU BLESSED ME, LORD…
THE LEAST I CAN DO IS
PRAISE YOU, LORD….

God is a Spirit of Light

God is life's reflecting pool, a Spirit
of Light...
He alone is peace and serenity, a holding
ground of joy!
He dissolves crushing pain and disperses
melancholic strain... the only way out of the
slush pile of living.
God through His son, Jesus is a leap onto
the attainable dream from disconsolations' bank.
Stranded where you are, with Him you can saunter to a
place of unintended luxury and unexpected tenderness...
The Lord God, Keeper of significant Brightness, is
a Spirit of Light.

"Consoled"

I am consoled by sentimental points and places seizing me,
delivering me to tenderness never experienced or felt. I never
realized pleasant appealing pastures or commanding passage
before now. In the silence of buried possibilities and passion I
was Everyman seeking to remedy the answer to the soulless
portion living deep inside-prepared to heave regret and fear into a
loveless, sound-proof background.
Don't expect for anything on the wings of life to blow on winds
of enormous universal sources and factors.
Sojourn with God, and His Son Jesus, let them light the way
through this darkened, unconquerable, earthbound flight.

"The Goodness of Life"

There are places I enjoy strolling toward,
marvelous discoveries in a step I come upon
in an instance, with a glance-a solitary tree waves
its mystery and magic……..
Deep, the marrow of life that overturns earths'
lusciousness to reveal unexpected joy…….

"A Wandering Light"

There's something there, translated in the wilderness of life… a wandering light, shallow in a space of time, escaped from a place of permanence-a roving minstrel singing rhyme, wispy and elusive in the mind, a current of universal goodness just around the bend, the Creators' wandering light, inspiration for all mankind.

"Silence and Solace Sought"

I look toward the magical points, the glistening
gems scattered throughout the universe....
Everyone's heart aims at harmlessness-
Warning signs shift the soul, and the spirit
lives in the whirling wind song...
Look, you've come far in the distant strange
harmonies, you are lost like fallen leaves...
In backward glances you preview silence
and solace sought......

"A Marvelous Breezy Concoction"

Something captures my soul from a faraway place,
carried on soft, summer breezes.....
I inherit an experience that has no location, nevertheless
currents of wind fashioned, soothe my spirit...
I am in the aftermath of life, suspended in a lingering
moment brewed in a tender wonderland with winds of
love stolen to capitulate yearning.

"Seeking, Seeking"

I am happy abandoned in browning leaves,
I enjoy gliding into the town of yearning-
to that simplistic and serene environ—
I await the place where joy resides.
I've seen my spirit torn to pieces.
Lucky are those who live in fields of grain.

"Lost World"

A culture of contentment seems to stir around me, taking me
to a mysterious plain, drawing me into places framed by
soundless, satisfying calm.....
Yearning and wistfulness capture my spirit on this evening
of solidifying shade and light....
I am transferred to halls and grounds and shores cloaked with a
lingering termless, timeless space and with a single quickening
glance, the lost world comes and goes.

"The Hilltop Call"

We throw away saving rituals for the
ravaging world…
and now, we fall into the sorcerer's
hands. We end up alone, lost in the
silence of darkness, harkening in the
wilds…
from somewhere I hear the call, the
lift I need beckoning with my desires
from a pleasant, satisfying hilltop…

"The Colorful Gaze of Autumn"

Oh the sense of wonderment and joy suspending
these warm autumn days…everything is an exponent
of God, created by nature's colorful gaze…..
Seeping through me from the sun-stroked trees is a smooth,
calm persuasion, like a seaside breeze…
I am filled with Goodness by this glimpse of God's Fullness.
As Nature shares its gloriousness, I could cry out with joyousness
when dark passages fall upon trees, emptying their flower-colored leaves.
As nature recesses in autumn-time, I recline in
shadowy corridor, and venture to be richly consumed.

Stranded In Life

I seek those tracts of time with no gage, perpetuating a soundless
memory in recognition of idyllic thought that to gaze will unfurl.
I was in a capsule of innocence and willingness…
It was a period of the undisclosed future,
before the schisms and failure, waiting-
I now find myself at those locations,
having traveled to those paths.
Curiously, nothing warns of life's true
difficulties ahead, the past holds a re-
collection of innocent light, glimpses inside
timid horizons.
I turn to mystery in this bold atmosphere as someone wistful,
prepared to hurl at pleasure never received of joyous
instances repressed in my thoughts and expectations.
The indefinable adversarial force idles, while
I appeal to the disrespectful goal present in living to STOP!

GOD'S HOLY LIGHT

I revel in this wayward time, distant life mingling with
rhyme…upon a
dim-filled, slumbering day, my mind is seized by this
display.…following
reveries' deep, deep trail, it is not possible to fail.
Familiar, am I with the outskirts of life…plus, I exist
with immense isolation.
I have the marvelous experience of being in the palm
of the open sky…
I like to look into the sanctuary of nature, to that place
which survives beyond view.
There is in everybody's time, a place lost, and rediscovered,
and I enjoy peering into that sacred, hallowed ground.
Simplicity, peace and serenity bound up, persuade and
enrich my spirit, aiming me toward a place of permanence
and restfulness.
My spirit gets renewed by glimpses and
visions of places and spaces filled with God's Holy Light.

A HAUNTING INLET

This particular inlet is a desolate, ominous place with unremitting silence, and where the stench of death and decay fills the atmosphere. It is an evening in spring, the time when the Horseshoe crab comes to the Delaware shores to spawn and die. (The Horseshoe crab is a seafaring creature with a spiked head and a tank-like body and resembles a Viking in armor). The path to the inlet follows a narrow, dirt road flocked by tall, ink-tipped bulrush and sedge through tall fields of wheat, barley and corn. The ancient bodies of the Horseshoe crab cram the inlet's dark, murky waters and the pebbly shores are crowded with their carcasses. (It is a clamorous event with hundreds swimming, and clamoring to join Horseshoe crab that number in the thousands cluttering the stony beach).

A frail wooden pier stands a short distance away in the middle of the dark, active, dramatic waters. (The frail wooden pier seems to be a scale for the desertion of life, a helpless structure there in the passive surreal drape covering the environment of the inlet. Inexplicably, the pier site turns my thoughts to shipwrecks, pirates' coves, coral reefs and even to damask tablecloths).

Nevertheless, the fragile pier is imperturbable, a kind of universal resistance standing there, with natural grace affirming it.

The isolated inlet seems to have journeyed from the moon, the cosmos or some archaic isle or even Pluto's Hell to claim this eternal location.

A COLONIAL TOWN HALL

One late-evening in spring I came upon a town hall in rural northern
Delaware that impressed me. Standing in magnificence and splendor
the Georgian brick structure reached back to the earliest colonists
engaged in discussions establishing America.
Like many historic buildings that recapitulate America's Colonial
Period by structure-Corinthian, Ionic, etc.-it constituted a
Horrendous revitalizing force.
Though moderate in size, its immense bearing circumscribed its
Natural origins. Beyond the patriotic significance emanating from
the town hall, this municipality amassed by darkness was a gem, a
glittering diamond, a small wonder.
Here, at this site, a blade of history seemed to cast its memory into
the surrounding's darkened woods.
At this location connecting me and the presence of a distant time
and place, immense consolation filled me as from a living stream,
dream.

REVELING IN WAYWARD TIME

I revel in this wayward time, distant life mingling with
rhyme…upon a
dim-filled, slumbering day, my mind is seized by this
display.…following
reveries' deep, deep trail, it is not possible to fail.
Familiar, am I with the outskirts of life…plus, I exist
with immense isolation.
I have the marvelous experience of being in the palm
of the open sky…
I like to look into the sanctuary of nature, to that place
which survives beyond view.
There is in everybody's time, a place lost, and rediscovered,
and I enjoy peering into that sacred, hallowed ground.
Simplicity, peace and serenity bound up, persuade and
enrich my spirit, aiming me toward a place of permanence
and restfulness, although I can only glimpse and savor its
vision for me.

THE HILLTOP CALL

We throw away saving rituals for the
ravaging world…
and now, we fall into the sorcerer's
hands. We end up alone, lost in the
silence of darkness, harkening in the
wilds…
from somewhere I hear the call, the
lift I need beckoning with my desires
from a pleasant, satisfying hilltop…

YOU'RE THE STAR OF MY HEART

YOU'RE THE STAR OF MY HEART...
YOU'RE THE STAR OF MY HEART...YOU'RE EVERY-
THING.....
YOU'RE THE SUN COMING, RISING OVER THE MOUN-
TAINS...
YOU BRING ME EVERYTHING...

YOU'RE THE SOOTHING SOUND OF RAIN...YOU'RE
EVERYTHING TO ME...
YOU'RE THE STAR OF MY HEART.. YOU'RE EVERY-
THING TO ME....

LOVE WAS WAITING TO CAPTURE MY HEART...AND
GIVE ME
EVERYTHING...
LOVE WAS WAITING FOR YOU...IT WAS STANDING IN
THE WING.....

YOU'RE THE STAR OF MY HEART...YOU'RE THE SUN
RISING OVER
THE MOUNTAINS....
YOU'RE THE SOOTHING SOUND OF RAIN...YOU'RE
EVERYTHING
TO ME...
YOU'RE THE STAR OF MY HEART........

"Inside of Silence"

A voluminous silence is transferring its difficult reproductions of life.
We're passing through deeply-troubled waters...images and
visions of Light and Hope have been weakened. I Thank You,
Lord for the capacity to endure and rise above the destructive
waves, avoiding through Your Grace the total disasters for self
and soul what sinful nature has wrought.
You, Jesus, have brought us safely over crossroads....
Your Spirit lifts us to joy from unexpected dangers and toils,
I could not trust life stretched before the paths I view without
Your shield against the fraudulent mystery and magic of living-the
nothingness of life without you.
God, inside of silence Your Majestic Grand Will stays in my gaze.

A WANDERING LIGHT

There's something there, translated in the wilderness of life… a wandering light, shallow in a space of time, escaped from a place of permanence-a roving minstrel singing rhyme, wispy and elusive in the mind, a current of universal goodness just around the bend, the Creators' wandering light, inspiration for all mankind.

"Reveling In Wayward Time"

I revel in this wayward time, distant life mingling with
rhyme…upon a
dim-filled, slumbering day, my mind is seized by this
display….following
reveries' deep, deep trail, it is not possible to fail.
Familiar, am I with the outskirts of life…plus, I exist
with immense isolation.
I have the marvelous experience of being in the palm
of the open sky…
I like to look into the sanctuary of nature, to that place
which survives beyond view.
There is in everybody's time, a place lost, and rediscovered,
and I enjoy peering into that sacred, hallowed ground.
Simplicity, peace and serenity bound up, persuade and
enrich my spirit, aiming me toward a place of permanence
and restfulness, although I can only glimpse and savor its
vision for me.

"A Poet"

A writer/poet has been given the gift to
Channel the universe, the dark depths circling
life, love, reality, everyone and everything.
In other words, the writer/poet's job is to describe
the subtle, silent places, the stored away magic and
mystery calling him or her to empty the heart and
mind into the dark, forlorn forest, the space capsule of life.
A writer/poet I find I'm explaining myself, stranded in life.

Loneliness-Melancholy's Strange Cradle

Loneliness is melancholy's strange cradle; lidless, estranged,
empty eyes. Horizons sparse, spread with vigilant tracts of
discouragement- a symbol of renegade posts, outposts,
plains full-proofed with indifference and atmospheres
dark with fluid shade and shadows.
Dejection, rejection, sentimentality, a thin ray of hope flushed away.
Uncrowned, drowned spirit, Hope will arrive like the dawn!

"Walk Behind God's Faithful Lead"

With all of the concerns we might have, don't let anything
shut you down, know that Hope is waiting
and desiring to be found.
Place all your Trust in Jesus, for Him to help you out....
He is the Only Answer against all fear and doubt,
He'll manage all your problems just allow him to take hold...
for then relief is on the way as you He will enfold.
The Lord is there for all you need, walk behind God's Faithful
Lead.

"A Black Soldier Man Sings Irish Melodies"

In the Army way back when, my buddy was tall, black and thin….
With the Irish lie his empathies, and often he would
sing their melodies.
So, whenever ale he did imbibe, songs of Ireland he'd describe.
Drowned in drink his hard voice would sing, in saddest tones
a bad voice can bring, all about the Erin race,
as tears came streaming down his face.
Tis better sounds from a tin can, than songs from
a tall, black thin soldier man.

"An English Landscape"

An English landscape seemed to weep,
as if primordial waters seep…
a location set in ancient brine and mystery,
evolved from archaic times-Westminster Abbey,
the Thames, Windsor Castle and places much revered…
then sightings of fairies,
gnomes and elves appeared.

"His Magnificence"

His magnificence imparts the perfected passage for a fractured humanity!
Move against the irreverent, unholy strains that would pull you from His purpose for this earthly experience.
Trust in the Lord to convert you from this mortal ground to Life Eternal.
Believe in the 'Possibility' ground into the Human spirit.
Have Faith, and daily challenge the Cause you represent.

"Hope Lures Across Life's Landscape"

Even in this season when the surroundings display autumn 's color and brilliance, society is held captive by a dark, debilitating, heavy, draining, disastrous spirit. However, in this autumnal landscape, hope lures.

In view of a colorful palette, I sublet my spirit to silent, arresting beauty on this autumn day. And in the presence of nature, and God's Glorious Light hope lures across life's landscape.

"What a Grand Purpose, Life"

Send complexities and difficulties
away to a distant shore.
Gods' tender, consoling spirit can enrich your being
fully.
Then no havoc can invade to collect your soul.
Serve a solid motive aligned with His love and
peace.
Don't be conformed to the destruction and cruelty
living presents.
Be lifted through the Lord's offering of 'goodness',
then what a Grand Purpose, Life!

LOSE YOURSELF TO GOD

We sometimes feel overwhelmed by life, I know I do. And in those troubling times, if I didn't know the Lord I would become a victim of despair and depression.

I am guaranteed help for all my troubles because I believe in Jesus Christ, God's only Son. Through the Holy Spirit, all my worries are vanquished. With Him we can work through our trials when we are challenged, He is in charge of All things.

No matter how deeply-troubled you are, remember, your Deep Faith translates into His Peace.

"The Unholy Dark Force" ("Be Transformed")

Life seems near monumental tragedy, yet a 'Shattering Truth' grips my mind....
We're on a collision course with fatality, marvelous though living could be....
Earth and nature's storms yield our thoughts to unforeseen, unprovoked, unannounced danger.....
The elastic, soothed spirit unprotected, feels stilted in the grave's huge threatening measure...
Against the catastrophic darkness we are but 'Ants' running about, awaiting the mammoth foot to stomp, or the bear's, cougar's, puma's attack; or the gulp of the python, alligator, crocodile; or the fall from a mountain's cliff,
or the floods; or the knife; gunfire; or the fire, or the.......
In the face of all of the baffling, frightening episodes harboring life, stretched before us, put the Lord in Charge
Be Transformed.

"Solidarity with the Lord"

Calamity seems on our doorstep! Life is over-flowing with disaster and detriment. We're perplexed, confounded in hostile surroundings. We're living in a chaotic, malfunctioning world. What I've mentioned, and more applies to life today.

Has mankind stretched a bridge too far? Have our miss-calculated actions caused the horrific, harrowing experience through which we're having to solemnly walk? Who knows!

I know about a 'Shelter' for atrocities and suffering of all kind you can claim— 'Solidarity with the Lord'!

"Consoled"

I am consoled by sentimental points and places seizing me,
delivering me to tenderness never experienced or felt. I never
realized pleasant appealing pastures or commanding passage
before now. In the silence of buried possibilities and passion I
was Everyman seeking to remedy the answer to the soulless
portion living deep inside-prepared to heave regret and fear into a
loveless, sound-proof background.
Don't expect for anything on the wings of life to blow against
winds of enormous universal sources and factors.
Sojourn with God, and His Son Jesus, let them Light the way
through this darkened, unconquerable, earthbound flight!

"Sharing my Springtime Thoughts"

The other day, my eyes caught a mother bird gather some twigs and fly off to build a nest. And looking around I saw spring coming alive in the budding trees and greenery, and blooming day lilies. From my backyard I viewed a lofty green heavily-branched evergreen seeming to harbor a deep placid existence. But it was looking into the prevailing sunlight in the surroundings beyond my home this morning that I realized the preponderance of what I'd witnessed this Springtime. It was the presence of the Lord's intrinsic Light, His Holy governance over nature, and over all.

THE CROSS TO THE PRESENT

Because Jesus Christ died on the cross we live with His spirit in us. Through His suffering and dying we are able to confront the ravages of life. He has made our burdens light.

God sent His only Son, Jesus Christ to die a horrible death on our behalf. He had seen enough of the wicked nature of this world, and the suffering of His children on earth. We are in constant battle with a world trying to alienate us from Him and the protection He provides.

From the Cross to the present we have been absolved of all of our wrong doings. Because of Salvation we were given through the tremendous sacrifice of our Lord and Savior Jesus Christ we are safe from world assault and damnation. It is through our Faith in Him that we can overcome the sorrow, grief and misery concentrated all around us.

AN APPEALLING SNOWY GRAY BACK-GROUND

I relish the call of life in the snowy gray background,
Nature’s matter that I view.
A quiet sight echoes, amid chaos I have found.
I experience a good measure of coping tucked in
the distance and all ‘round.
I’m transported in the arms of a
peaceful snowy gray background.

A CRITICAL LOOK AT FEBRUARY

A critical look at 'February' means we will get to know…
January's gone, with some of its ice and snow…
Deep, shadowy…and silent as a dorm….
(twist December's solstice and March's equinox), it's
Winter's darkest form…..
Raven-black and somber, it can appear bereft…and have
the haunting presence some middle-earth has left…
A posture on its landscape can open Cupid's door…
Indeed February's no dark stranger any more…
Legacies of pride it has, like Martin Luther King….
February's optimism gets brightened up by Spring.

"Life Isn't the Same"

For certain, 2020 presented a feeling of overall Disaster—almost a sense of 'unworldliness' with its dispositioning wrecking crew effect on society.

We are all aware of the destructive outbreaks, one thing on top of the other we had to confront-the Corona Virus, the racial unrest, the United States 'Elections', plus other disabling and destructive matters and issues installed during the year 2020.

Life as we knew it became transformed by a strange, dark invasion. Pathologically and spiritually normal society fell under the covering of a virulent formation. It felt impossible to refute such a horrendous imposition I call a 'Wrecking Ball'.

Nevertheless, the 'Christmas' season arrived playing an enervating role, a time celebrating the birth of Christ Jesus, a time on earth for joy, hope, and peace. The birth of Jesus Christ is a reminder to the world that He can overturn the burdensome disposition hovering overall—rejoice and be encouraged.

A MESSAGE OF ENCOURAGEMENT IN THESE CALAMITOUS, DISMAYING TIMES

It might seem we're on a journey fraught with degradation, division, hurt, harm, darkness, danger. Nonetheless, we're humans on an earthly sun-glazed trail, entrenched in God's Bright Hope!

THE WRITER'S PATH

A writer has been given the gift to channel the universe, the dark depths circling life, love, reality, everyone and everything. In other words, a writer's job is to describe the subtle, silent places, the stored away magic and mystery calling him or her to empty into the dark, forlorn forest…the space of the heart and mind, the life capsule.

The writer possesses a plaintive song, a dream of aspiration, consolation, knowledge, inspiration and optimism to interpret, and pour into a world culture.

Writers have a purpose to energetically use every stretch of their imagination, and be disciplined as they engage the flow of creativity circling life.

www.ingramcontent.com/pod-product-compliance
Lightning Source LLC
Chambersburg PA
CBHW050025170726
48282CB00025B/547

* 9 7 8 8 1 8 2 5 3 8 6 7 2 *